John Cena Beyond the Wrestling Ring

A Biography Of John Cena, A
Phenomenon That Transcended
Wrestling, A Journey Of Triumph,
Impact, And Hustle, Loyalty, Respect

Michael P. Poore

Table of Contents

Introduction

In the annals of professional wrestling history, many names resound not just inside the boundaries of the squared circle but also in the larger domain of popular culture. John Cena, a name that has become associated with tenacity, charm, and flexibility, stands as a defining character in the world of professional wrestling and entertainment at large. With an effect that stretches well beyond the ropes, Cena's journey from a youthful dreamer to a worldwide legend has left an everlasting impression on the business and the hearts of millions.

The roots of Cena's impact can be traced back to a period when the wrestling scene was experiencing a transition. As the 20th century gave way to the 21st, the planned drama and athleticism of professional wrestling started to fascinate a broader audience, blurring the borders between sport and entertainment. It was against this developing background that John Cena emerged, not just as a tremendous athlete but also as a charming showman who would redefine what it meant to be a wrestling superstar.

Cena's ascension was more than simply a product of his in ring skill; it was a perfect confluence of character, talent, and timing. Debuting in the cutthroat world of WWE (World Wrestling Entertainment) in the early 2000s, Cena's first image as a youthful and brash rapper   the "Doctor of Thuganomics"   was a breath of new air. His freestyle raps and unabashed attitude poured new energy into the wrestling industry, laying the groundwork for what would become a renowned career.

However, Cena could grow that ultimately established his position in the pantheon of wrestling legends. As the crowd evolved, so did Cena. The "Doctor of Thuganomics" morphed into the epitome of "Hustle, Loyalty, Respect," a motto that resonated with both the devoted devotees and the casual viewers. His character's journey from a rebellious rapper to a paragon of virtue highlighted his incredible adaptability and determination to reinvent himself.

Cena's effect expanded beyond the staged realm of wrestling narratives. His larger than life presence transcended the ring and made its way into different sectors of entertainment. Hollywood beckoned, and Cena heeded the call with the same determination that catapulted him to championship triumph. His venture into acting saw him appearing in blockbuster blockbusters, smoothly transferring from the canvas of the wrestling arena to the silver screen. This changeover wasn't just about novelty; it was a tribute to Cena's ability to command attention, regardless of the media.

Beyond the spectacle and the accolades, John Cena's bond with his fans propelled him to a unique tier of success. His presence, both physical and figurative, became a light of hope for many. His persistent efforts outside the ring, notably his work with the Have A Wish Foundation, highlighted his humility and genuine desire to have a good influence on lives far distant from the limelight. Cena's charity initiatives reinforced the concept that heroes exist not just in the domain of fiction but also in the lives of people they touch.

In an age when the internet can convert events into memes, Cena's catchphrases and signature gestures developed a life of their own in the digital sphere. The "John Cena" meme, marked by his surprising arrival with the burst of trumpets, further reinforced his popularity as a pop cultural hero. This phenomenon embodied the universality of his appeal, a character that could be admired, mocked, and mimicked by fans and non fans alike.

The effect of John Cena on professional wrestling and entertainment cannot be reduced to a unique story. His path illustrates the dynamic character of celebrity in the current day, where a wrestler may transform into a global ambassador, an actor can reverberate as a wrestling legend, and a catchphrase can transcend decades. Cena's tale is not only about contrived rivalries and written wins; it's about the very real victories he's accomplished, the lives he's touched, and the hearts he's won.

As we go into the chapters of John Cena's life, it becomes evident that his effect on professional wrestling and entertainment extends beyond titles and box office revenues. It's about inspiration, reinvention, and the irresistible charm that has captivated the globe. Cena's legacy is an enduring tribute to the force of a desire followed by unrelenting determination, a spirit that continues to inspire both the wrestling ring and the international stage.

Chapter 1

Early Life and Wrestling Beginnings

In the fabric of legends, every journey has a beginning, and for John Cena, the roots of his incredible narrative go back to his early upbringing and his unshakable devotion to the world of professional wrestling. From modest origins to the edge of celebrity, this chapter unravels the formative years of a man who would go on to reinvent sports entertainment.

Childhood and Upbringing

John Felix Anthony Cena Jr. was born on April 23, 1977, in West Newbury, Massachusetts, to Carol and John Cena Sr.

Raised in a family of Italian and French Canadian roots, Cena's youth was anchored on ideals of hard labour, discipline, and family ties. His father, a former wrestling announcer, exposed him to the world of wrestling at an early age, laying the scenario for the seeds of enthusiasm to be sowed.

Growing up with four brothers, Cena acquired a competitive drive that would later serve him well in the realm of wrestling. His parents stressed the value of education, and Cena excelled academically, even winning a Division III All American football accolades during his high school years. His agility and attention to his academics demonstrated the balance that would become a trademark of his later career.

Early Passion for Wrestling

While his scholastic aspirations were promising, it was the attraction of wrestling that ultimately stole Cena's heart. Inspired by the larger than life characters and dramatic confrontations he observed on television, Cena's goal of becoming a professional wrestler started to take form. This idea, however, was not only a whimsical thought; it was a calling that propelled him to pursue ways to convert it into reality.

Training at Ultimate Pro Wrestling's Ultimate University

Determined to put his passion into a real route, Cena sought out professional instruction that would shape him into a wrestler capable of controlling the ring. He enrolled in the Ultimate Pro Wrestling's Ultimate University, a famous training facility that has produced countless wrestling stars. Under the tutelage of seasoned specialists, Cena underwent intense training that challenged his physical and mental strength.

His time at Ultimate University was marked by tough exercises, technical drills, and a focus on developing the art of storytelling via wrestling. Cena's passion showed as he accepted the obstacles with an unwavering drive to improve his trade. This aspect of his career was essential in developing his foundation as a wrestler and entertainer.

OVW and the "OVW 4"

Cena's rigorous training and commitment finally led him to Ohio Valley Wrestling (OVW), a developing territory for WWE. Here, he continued to polish his abilities under the direction of seasoned instructors. Cena's charm and natural skill did not go unnoticed; he rapidly emerged as a standout star among OVW's ranks.

The OVW tenure was notable not just for Cena's evolution as a wrestler but also for the critical alliance that would influence his early career direction. Cena, together with other aspiring wrestlers Randy Orton, Brock Lesnar, and Batista, created a clique known as the "OVW 4." This alliance highlighted their talent and predicted the effect they would collectively have on the major stage of professional wrestling.

The "OVW 4" underlined Cena's ability to flourish in a competitive setting while creating friendships with his teammates. The experience not only cemented his in ring talents but also provided the basis for the friendships and rivalries that would become essential to his path when he migrated to WWE's main roster.

In the crucible of childhood ambitions, early influences, and diligent training, John Cena's road to wrestling success was distinguished by a dedication that was as unbreakable as it was honourable. The marriage of his passion, background, and the guidance he got throughout his early years prepared the road for his ascension to the top of sports entertainment. As Chapter 1 finishes, the scene is set for Cena's debut on the greatest platform of them all, where he would begin writing his name into the annals of wrestling history.

Chapter 2

Rise to Fame

Debut in WWE and Early Appearances

John Cena's emergence on the great platform of WWE heralded the commencement of a stratospheric ascension that would forever reshape the world of professional wrestling. As he went into the squared circle of WWE, little did the world realise that they were about to witness the birth of an icon. This chapter goes into Cena's earliest steps inside the WWE world, his transformation from a rookie to a force to be reckoned with, and the lasting impression he made on sports entertainment.

Cena's debut in WWE occurred on the June 27, 2002, edition of "SmackDown!" when he answered an open challenge by Kurt Angle, an established and renowned figure in the wrestling business. Despite being relatively unknown at the time, Cena's charm, athleticism, and unflinching confidence soon attracted the attention of fans and critics alike. Even in loss, Cena's performance demonstrated his potential to become a future star.

Adoption of the "Doctor of Thuganomics" Persona

In the domain of professional wrestling, the capacity to adapt and change is an essential attribute. Cena spectacularly displayed this by changing from a bland babyface character to the dynamic "Doctor of Thuganomics." This metamorphosis let Cena tap into his innate humour, charm, and skill for freestyle rapping. Embracing a loud attitude, he exhibited a distinct combination of confidence and irreverence that distinguished him from his contemporaries.

The "Doctor of Thuganomics" moniker not only demonstrated Cena's flexibility but also connected emotionally with the shifting cultural milieu of the early 2000s. His freestyle raps became a vital part of his persona, offering a forum for him to communicate with the audience in a way that surpassed conventional wrestling tales.

This growth was important in establishing Cena as a star performer and a fan favourite.

Feuds and Rivalries that Propelled His Career

A wrestler's road to superstardom is generally distinguished by the rivalries they participate in, and John Cena's career was no different. His ability to build interesting feuds and rivalries played a significant part in boosting his career to unparalleled heights. One such feud that left an enduring imprint was his duel with Eddie Guerrero.

Cena's fight with Guerrero not only showed his in ring skills but also displayed his talent to craft emotionally charged storylines inside the wrestling arena. The contrast between Guerrero's crafty techniques and Cena's relentless tenacity generated a dramatic storyline that grabbed spectators. This battle demonstrated Cena's flexibility, as he shifted from the comedic antics of the "Doctor of Thuganomics" to a more serious and determined adversary.

Another significant conflict that aided Cena's growth was his fierce battle with Brock Lesnar. The collision of Cena's perseverance with Lesnar's physical power resulted in memorable encounters that demonstrated Cena's ability to flourish in high stakes scenarios. This feud further reinforced Cena's image as a top tier talent and a cornerstone of WWE's roster.

Cena's ascension was also highlighted by his feud with JBL (John "Bradshaw" Layfield), which culminated in a heated duel for the WWE Championship at WrestleMania 21. This battle of characters and ideals highlighted Cena's ability to bear the weight of main event contests on the greatest platform, further confirming his standing as a marquee draw.

In the crucible of the wrestling ring, Cena's feuds and rivalries were not merely fought for power; they were narrative canvases onto which he painted storylines that connected with spectators on a fundamental level. His ability to generate emotional connections via his performances boosted him from a promising rookie to a real superstar, laying the way for his transformational effect on sports entertainment.

Chapter 3

Championship Reigns and Main Event Status

Evolution of Character and Wrestling Style

As John Cena's career maintained its upward trend, his demeanour and wrestling style experienced a makeover that confirmed his place as a sports entertainment legend. Chapter 3 looks into the transformational part of Cena's career, covering how he modified his image and in ring technique to capture spectators and become a household figure.

Cena's development was a tribute to his ability to adapt and connect with various audiences. The transformation from the arrogant "Doctor of Thuganomics" to a patriotic and inspiring figure displayed his versatility as a performer. Embracing the character of the all American hero, Cena leaned upon his own ideals and charm to appeal to fans of all ages. His "Never Give Up" credo became a rallying cry, expressing fortitude in the face of hardship and connecting with supporters fundamentally.

Simultaneously, Cena's wrestling technique also developed. He developed his technical talents, integrated a varied variety of movements, and became recognized for his unique moves, including the Attitude Adjustment and the STF (Stepover Toehold

Facelock). This growth was distinguished by a concentration on storytelling inside the ring, demonstrating his ability to express emotions and storylines via his fights. Cena's ring psychology and ability to captivate the crowd transformed his bouts from basic contests to riveting dramas that made a lasting impression.

Record Breaking Championship Wins

A feature of Cena's career was his incredible championship wins. He continuously elevated championship belts into emblems of respect and honour, and his record breaking reigns underlined his power inside WWE. This portion of the chapter discusses his historic championship triumphs and the importance of each success.

Cena's pursuit of title success achieved a critical milestone as he claimed his first WWE title at WrestleMania 21. This triumph heralded the beginning of a succession of extraordinary championship reigns that would define his legend. Cena's ability to continually acquire and defend championships highlighted his perseverance, drive, and devotion to perfection.

One of the most remarkable successes of Cena's career was his unparalleled 16 time WWE World Championship reign, a record he shares with the great Ric Flair. This feat not only established his position in wrestling history but also emphasised his ability to stay relevant and compelling over a lengthy time.

Headlining WrestleMania and Other Major Events

Cena's climb to main event prominence culminated in his involvement in the greatest stages of them all: WrestleMania and other major events. These displays were not only chances to flaunt his in ring skills but also platforms to deliver engaging tales that connected with worldwide audiences. This section dives into Cena's WrestleMania moments and his contributions to WWE's largest yearly extravaganza.

Cena's WrestleMania trip was highlighted by his confrontation with some of the industry's top personalities, including The Rock, Triple H, and Shawn Michaels. His WrestleMania 23 clash against Shawn Michaels in a boat called "The Battle of the Billionaires' ' was a marvel in narrative. The emotional engagement, technical excellence, and sheer intensity of their meeting underlined Cena's capacity to perform on the largest platform.

Equally memorable was Cena's rivalry with The Rock, which resulted in two consecutive WrestleMania big events. These fights between two generational superstars encapsulated the spirit of WWE's history and present, grabbing worldwide attention and pushing the frontiers of sports entertainment.

Beyond WrestleMania, Cena's participation headlined several important events, including SummerSlam, Royal Rumble, and Survivor Series. His presence in these shows added to their grandeur and reinforced his standing as a headlining attraction.

Chapter 4

Character Transformations

Transition to the "Superman" Persona

This chapter dives into a critical chapter of John Cena's career defined by his shift to the "Superman" identity. This period demonstrated Cena's transformation from a conventional heroic character to a modern day paragon of perseverance and everlasting loyalty. The chapter discusses how this shift reshaped his persona and further reinforced his prominence as a larger than life presence in the realm of professional wrestling.

John Cena's transition into the "Superman" image may be credited to his ability to connect with spectators on a fundamental level. As he went from being a defiant rapper and rebellious figure, he eventually accepted a more wholesome and aspirational one. The metamorphosis was not a simple cosmetic adjustment; it signified Cena's desire to inspire and empower his followers, beyond the bounds of the squared circle.

The "Superman" persona was distinguished by its focus on virtuous principles, fortitude in the face of adversities, and an unshakeable devotion to doing what is right. Cena's presentation of this character stretched beyond planned storylines—it became an extension of his own views and attitude on life. His true devotion to practising the ideas he taught connected strongly with his supporters, turning him into a real life role model.

Embracing the "Hustle, Loyalty, Respect" Motto

At the centre of Cena's change was the renowned motto: "Hustle, Loyalty, Respect." This phrase not only defined Cena's persona but also represented the spirit of his journey. The chapter dives into the origins and importance of each component of this phrase, explaining how it became a guiding concept for Cena both within and beyond the wrestling ring.

"Hustle" reflected Cena's persistent work ethic and his determination to continually strive for perfection. It expressed his commitment to give his best in every performance, representing the attitude of tenacity and devotion.

"Loyalty" referred to Cena's undying loyalty to his fans, his coworkers, and the profession he had committed his life to. His commitment was obvious in his regular presence, his interaction with the WWE Universe, and his dedication to charity initiatives.

"Respect" formed the cornerstone of Cena's dealings with both opponents and friends. His display of respect proved that although he was a fierce opponent, he preserved a code of honour and sportsmanship. This facet of his persona connected with people and led to his tremendous appeal.

Shift to a More Polarising Figure Among Fans

As Cena's persona developed, so did the fan responses to him. What started as near universal love later morphed into a more divisive reaction. Chapter 4 addresses this transformation, exploring how Cena's prominence as a role model and continuous presence at the top of the card led to conflicting opinions from the WWE Universe.

Cena's elevation to a more divisive character was an inevitable byproduct of his ongoing success and widespread presence. While he continued to have a committed fan following, a segment of the audience started to show disagreement. Some fans sought variation and diversity in the main event scenario, resulting in a "mixed reaction" phenomenon where applause and boos coexisted during Cena's entrances.

The divisiveness was further fanned by the "Cena Wins LOL" meme, which playfully pointed out his habit of emerging triumphant in high stakes matches. While originally a funny comment, it added to the notion that Cena was "overpowered" and unstoppable, motivating some fans to cheer against him as a form of resistance.

Chapter 5

Beyond the Ring From Wrestling to Hollywood

In the annals of sports entertainment history, few people have managed to transcend the limitations of the wrestling ring and have a big effect on the realm of Hollywood entertainment. John Cena, already a known WWE superstar, began a spectacular journey that carried him from the squared circle to the big screen. "Beyond the Ring From Wrestling to Hollywood," follows Cena's development from a wrestling superstar to a versatile Hollywood celebrity, displaying his incredible flexibility and ambition to explore new boundaries.

Pursuit of an Acting Career

John Cena's introduction into the realm of acting wasn't only a casual journey. It was a deliberate move inspired by his ambition, work ethic, and desire to explore new possibilities for artistic expression. This chapter dives into Cena's early interest in acting and the actions he took to set the framework for a successful shift.

Cena's path in the acting field started with tiny parts and cameo appearances, enabling him to dip his toes into the waters of the entertainment business. These early experiences not only provided him with great exposure but also enabled him to learn from seasoned experts in the sector. Cena's desire to start from the bottom and his openness to learning displayed his humility and resolve to earn his position in a new arena.

Roles in Movies and Television Shows

Cena's acting career gained momentum as he earned parts in several movies and television series. The chapter discusses the variety of personalities he represented and the breadth of genres he explored. From action packed blockbusters to comedies and tragedies, Cena's willingness to take on various parts emphasised his flexibility as an actor.

One important facet of Cena's acting career was his ability to imbue his performances with the same charm and honesty that had endeared him to wrestling fans. This chapter covers major roles that highlight Cena's ability to connect with audiences outside the wrestling arena. Whether he was playing a tough Marine, a humorous foil, or a serious role, Cena's on screen presence remained fascinating and engaging.

Transitioning from Wrestling to Hollywood

Cena's move from wrestling to Hollywood was not without its hurdles. The chapter discusses how Cena handled his responsibilities to both WWE and his blossoming film career. It digs into the physical and emotional challenges of his two responsibilities, giving light to the complicated balancing act he managed to maintain.

His transformation was not just a personal milestone but also a profound societal movement. Cena's breakthrough in Hollywood destroyed the myth that wrestlers could only find success inside the limits of the wrestling profession. He became an inspiration to young wrestlers and entertainers who wished to extend their horizons and seek different paths for their abilities.

As Cena's acting career progressed, he found himself appearing in huge blockbuster series and leading movies, gaining fans not just because of his wrestling celebrity but also due to his true acting talents. The chapter finishes by commenting on the influence Cena's popularity had on transforming the attitudes of wrestlers in the entertainment business.

John Cena's unwavering dedication and his ability to make a smooth transition from the realm of professional wrestling to the glitter and glamour of Hollywood. His pursuit of an acting profession, his numerous roles in film and television, and his successful transfer all illustrate his potential to flourish in many fields. Cena's journey from the wrestling ring to the big screen serves as an inspirational narrative of reinvention and a tribute to the unlimited potential of those who dare to dream beyond their early accomplishments.

Chapter 6

Philanthropy and Impact John Cena's Benevolent Legacy

In the domain of showbiz, where recognition frequently becomes a pedestal for selfish indulgence, John Cena's narrative takes a joyful turn. "Philanthropy and Impact," dives into Cena's strong devotion to make a positive influence in the lives of others. Beyond the flash and glamour of the wrestling ring and Hollywood, Cena's charity initiatives shine brightly as a tribute to his character and the permanent impression he has made on the world.

John Cena's Contributions to Charitable Causes

John Cena's path from professional wrestling to Hollywood was paralleled by a parallel one of giving back to society. This chapter analyses how Cena's popularity and influence became a driving reason behind his charity activities. It outlines his engagement with a broad variety of humanitarian initiatives, indicating his genuine desire to utilise his platform for the greater good.

Cena's donations went well beyond giving cheques or donating his name. He devoted his time, energy, and resources to efforts that fit with his principles. Whether it was helping education, healthcare, or disaster relief operations, Cena's devotion to having a good effect was both visible and profound. This chapter covers various philanthropic organisations and initiatives that Cena championed, offering insight into the breadth of his commitment.

Work with Make A Wish Foundation

Perhaps one of the most touching elements of Cena's altruism was his engagement with the Make A Wish Foundation. Cena's contacts with youngsters battling grave diseases reflect the real compassion and sensitivity that characterise his character. This chapter dives into the enormous influence Cena had on the lives of these children and their families.

Cena's passion for the Make A Wish Foundation extends much beyond sporadic appearances. He holds the record for fulfilling the most wishes via the foundation, a monument to his steadfast devotion to delivering joy and hope to individuals facing hard situations. The chapter relates moving accounts of Cena's meetings with wish recipients, highlighting the significant and enduring influence he had on their lives.

Advocacy for Social Issues

Cena's charity endeavours weren't restricted to typical nonprofit groups. He also utilised his position to speak for social problems near to his heart. This chapter highlights how Cena uses his position to promote awareness about key problems, like education, diversity, and social equality.

Cena's activism expanded to public speaking engagements, media appearances, and the usage of his social media networks. He wasn't hesitant to offer his voice to issues that mattered, frequently urging others to join the discourse and take action. His ability to bridge the gap between his celebrity position and his genuine concern for society concerns made his advocacy both legitimate and influential.

John Cena's legacy as a humanitarian and a kind human being. His donations to humanitarian organisations, his transformational work with the Make A

Wish Foundation, and his advocacy for social concerns all present a picture of a man who exploited his power for the welfare of mankind. Cena's charity extends beyond cash gifts; it represents a strong appreciation of the power one person may have to inspire change and bring optimism to the lives of others. His beneficent legacy serves as a reminder that genuine effect is defined not only by personal successes but also by the difference one makes in the lives of others in need.

Chapter 7

Memes and Pop Culture John Cena's Unexpected Online Stardom

In the ever evolving world of pop culture, there are instances when an individual's effect transcends their core area of expertise and becomes a phenomenon that resonates with a global audience. Chapter 7, titled "Memes and Pop Culture," dives into John Cena's surprising path from the wrestling arena to becoming an online celebrity and a ubiquitous presence in memes, establishing his reputation as a cultural icon.

John Cena's Internet Memes and Viral Moments

The internet has a tendency to shower unexpected notoriety onto people, sometimes for the most unorthodox reasons. John Cena found himself at the core of this phenomenon when his wrestling character became the topic of innumerable memes and viral videos. This chapter covers the roots of the "John Cena meme," tracking its rise from a specialised inside joke among wrestling enthusiasts to a broad online craze.

The meme often features a quick and raucous apparition of John Cena's visage or theme music, taking spectators by surprise. This unexpectedness formed the heart of the meme's comedy, and its simplicity made it accessible to a broad spectrum of people. The chapter dives into numerous variations of the meme, illustrating how it was ingeniously incorporated into multiple settings, ranging from internet forums to mainstream media.

Cultural Impact and Recognition Beyond Wrestling

While John Cena's origins lay in professional wrestling, his effect has gone well beyond the squared circle. This chapter discusses how his meme worthy moments led to his larger cultural awareness. Cena's visage and catchphrases became part of a bigger cultural debate, even among individuals who may not have been enthusiastic wrestling fans.

Furthermore, the meme's popularity worked as a bridge across generations. Older audiences that followed Cena's wrestling career found themselves accidentally participating in online culture, while newer generations discovered Cena via memes before diving into his wrestling history. This unanticipated cross generational relationship gave a new dimension to Cena's already diverse appeal.

Cena's ability to accept the meme, engage in the joke, and even produce self aware material shows his acute awareness of the current media ecosystem. His willingness to accept this online stardom with humility and humour further endeared him to a varied audience.

Chapter 8

Personal Life and Relationships

Marriages, Divorces, and Family Life

In the complicated fabric of a public figure's life, the domain of personal connections frequently provides a striking contrast to their public image. This chapter looks into the deep aspects of John Cena's personal life, including his marriages, divorces, and the subtleties of his family life.

John Cena's romantic relationships have been a source of substantial media interest. His high profile marriage to Elizabeth Huberdeau in 2009 gave a look into his personal life. However, the marriage finally ended in divorce in 2012, prompting conjecture and attention from both fans and media. This chapter navigates the difficulty of keeping a private relationship in the limelight and the influence of media intrusion on personal concerns.

Cena's subsequent relationship with fellow wrestler Nikki Bella garnered even more attention due to their shared fame and the reality television show "Total Divas." The proposal that took place at WrestleMania 33 captured the hearts of fans, yet the engagement eventually faced its own struggles and ended in 2018. Exploring the nuances of these relationships gives a glimpse into Cena's fragility and the difficulty of maintaining a personal life despite public scrutiny.

Public Persona vs. Private Life

One of the eternal mysteries of celebrities is the discrepancy between their public image and their off screen reality. This chapter dives into the dichotomy of John Cena's identity, both as the captivating wrestling superstar and as the guy yearning for a sense of normality away from the stadium lights.

Cena's public presence as a larger than life figure typically required embracing heroic attributes and strong moral ideals, which resonated with his wrestling fans. However, behind the scenes, Cena wrestled with the problem of keeping a sense of self under the expectations of stardom. This chapter discusses the conflict between maintaining an image that inspires others and creating opportunities for personal development and honesty.

Interests & Hobbies Outside of Wrestling

Beyond the noise of the audience and the intensity of the wrestling arena, people frequently seek refuge and pleasure in their inner pursuits. This chapter gives insight into John Cena's numerous interests and hobbies that transcend beyond his wrestling profession.

Cena's engagement in different charity projects displays his devotion to having a good effect on the world. His devotion to the

Make A Wish Foundation and other philanthropic organisations testifies to his character beyond the manufactured image of the ring. Additionally, Cena's venture into acting and his performances in movies reflect his drive to explore new creative possibilities.

Outside the limelight, Cena is an enthusiastic automobile aficionado, having a significant collection of cars. His enthusiasm for vehicles mirrors his curiosity about mechanics and design, allowing a look into the side of Cena that finds satisfaction in workmanship and engineering.

Chapter 9

Challenges and Comebacks

Injuries and Setbacks in His Wrestling Career

The route to success is sometimes littered with challenges, and John Cena's career in the realm of professional wrestling is no exception. This chapter dives into the challenges and tribulations he endured in the form of injuries and disappointments, which challenged his physical toughness and mental fortitude.

Throughout his stellar career, Cena had several ailments that impacted his ability to compete at the best level. From muscular strains to more significant ailments such as a torn pectoral muscle, these physical setbacks not only sidelined him but also forced him to face the frailty of his own body. This chapter highlights the toll that injuries had on his career, requiring him to step back from the limelight and participate in rigorous rehabilitation to restore his place in the wrestling hierarchy.

Resilience and Determination to Return

One of the distinguishing attributes of a real champion is the capacity to bounce back from adversity with unrelenting tenacity. John Cena's tenacity in the face of adversity served as an inspiration to fans and fellow wrestlers alike. This section goes into the attitude that enabled Cena to rise beyond injuries and failures, exhibiting a tenacious devotion to his trade and his fans.

Cena's drive to return stronger than before was a tribute to his work ethic and devotion. He persistently pushed himself through difficult healing procedures, exhibiting not just his physical tenacity but also his mental fortitude. His endurance became a source of encouragement for others, reminding them that failures are simply transitory barriers on the route to greatness.

Facing New and Emerging Talents

As the wrestling world grew, so did the array of talent that Cena shared the ring with.

This chapter highlights how Cena negotiated the shifting tides of the wrestling business, going up against a new generation of rivals trying to make their mark.

Cena's willingness to accept change and confront new talents proved his devotion to the progression of the sport. He participated in feuds with emerging stars, boosting their development while retaining his own standing as a regular in the wrestling business. His battles with talents like CM Punk, Seth Rollins, and Kevin Owens demonstrated his flexibility and his desire to put over the new generation of superstars.

Chapter 10

Legacy and Influence

Evaluation of Cena's Influence on the Wrestling Industry

John Cena's effect on the wrestling profession is significant and multi-faceted, spanning over two decades. This chapter dives deep into his impact, exploring how he transformed and remade the environment of professional wrestling.

Cena's impact is distinguished by his ability to connect with varied audiences. His captivating demeanour, paired with his unusual combination of athleticism and mic abilities, made him a global fan favourite.

He surpassed the usual bounds of wrestling fans, drawing not just long time devotees but also newbies to the sport. His popularity stretched beyond wrestling arenas, reaching homes across the globe via television screens, pay per view events, and internet platforms.

As a forerunner, Cena helped to the internationalisation of WWE. His popularity had a crucial part in increasing the company's reach into other markets, building a worldwide community of followers. His goods, catchphrases, and character became cultural touchstones, establishing his place as a pop culture star.

Comparison to Other Legendary Wrestlers

To comprehend Cena's legacy completely, it's vital to situate his triumphs within the greater spectrum of wrestling history. This portion of the text draws connections between Cena and other great personalities, stressing his specific achievements and the unique problems he encountered.

In the arena of professional wrestling, parallels are sometimes made to iconic superstars like Hulk Hogan, Stone Cold Steve Austin, and The Rock. Cena's impact, though, remains a tribute to his ability to manage shifting times and audiences. Unlike some of his predecessors, Cena's career spans decades defined by fluctuating fan tastes and technical breakthroughs. He effectively moved from the "Ruthless Aggression" phase to the Reality phase and beyond, proving his versatility and staying strong.

Cena's Lasting Impact on WWE and Entertainment

John Cena's influence reaches well beyond the wrestling arena. This section discusses his effect on WWE's trajectory and his involvement in changing the larger entertainment industry.

Within WWE, Cena's impact is visible in his contributions to the company's marketing strategy, commercial relationships, and branding activities. His marketability enhanced WWE's commercial appeal, gaining sponsorships, media attention, and partnerships that accelerated the organisation's financial success. Cena's passion for charities and his position as a goodwill ambassador also helped WWE's strong public image.

In the area of entertainment, Cena's shift from wrestling to Hollywood has reinforced his position as a dynamic performer. He successfully moved between the worlds of professional wrestling and acting, starring in a variety of movies and television series. His success in entertainment matches his ability to fascinate audiences, and his appearance on the silver screen propelled wrestling into popular discourse.

Conclusion

Reflecting on John Cena's Journey from Aspiring Wrestler to Global Icon

John Cena's path from a young and determined wrestler to a worldwide legend is a monument to the power of passion, determination, and the ability to connect with people on a fundamental level. As we close this biography, we reflect on the incredible arc of Cena's career, the influence he has had on the wrestling industry and beyond, and the timeless lessons that his narrative provides.

Cena's path is a classic narrative of ambitions turning into reality via pure devotion and hard effort. From his early days on the wrestling circuit to his record breaking title reigns in WWE, Cena has displayed an unshakeable commitment to his trade. This devotion wasn't restricted to the limits of the ring; it extended to his relationships with fans, his charity initiatives, and his ongoing progress as a performer.

One of the most astounding parts of Cena's career is his ability to grow with the times while remaining loyal to his fundamental ideals. He surfed the shifting tides of the wrestling business, modifying his character and style to connect with new generations of fans. From the boisterous "Doctor of Thuganomics" to the inspiring "Superman" persona, Cena's shifts paralleled his own maturation as a human. This versatility enabled him to stay current and appreciated by followers young and old.

Cena's effect stretches well beyond wrestling. His excursion into Hollywood is a tribute to his flexibility as a performer and his ability to transcend the confines of his first profession. Whether he's mesmerising spectators in the ring or on the big screen, Cena's presence demands attention. His passion for his acting assignments reflects his attitude to wrestling — he immerses himself entirely, continuously aiming to provide the finest performance possible.

Furthermore, Cena's charity endeavours highlight the depth of his character and his devotion to having a good influence on the world. His work with organisations like the

Make A Wish Foundation has given pleasure and inspiration to many lives. His support for social concerns shows his commitment to leveraging his platform for positive change, further reinforcing his reputation as a role model both inside and beyond the ring.

Reflecting on Cena's career also encourages us to evaluate the larger influence of professional wrestling as a cultural phenomenon. The sport has the unique capacity to generate larger than life personalities that engage strongly with fans. Cena's narrative highlights the power of storytelling, passion, and connection that wrestling can generate. His legendary catchphrases, historic rivalries, and unforgettable experiences have left an everlasting impression on the collective memory of fans.

In a world where the boundary between fact and fantasy sometimes blurs, Cena's ability to establish a true relationship with his audience stands out. He grasped the importance of his job not just as a performer but also as a symbol of hope, dedication, and positivism. This honesty is what propelled him from being a popular wrestler to a worldwide superstar.

As we complete John Cena's biography, we are left with a great respect for his contributions to the world of professional wrestling, entertainment, and charity. His path epitomises the core of what it means to seek one's ambitions persistently, to adapt and grow in the face of change, and to utilise one's influence for the welfare of others. John Cena's effect is not only a product of his successes; it's a result of the principles he stands for and the inspiration he brings to countless others throughout the globe. His narrative will continue to reverberate for centuries to come, reminding us all that with hard effort, persistence, and a true heart, we may truly climb to become idols in our own way.

Appendices

Appendix A: List of Championships and Achievements

John Cena's career has been decorated with multiple titles and awards that confirm his place as one of the most successful and beloved wrestlers in the history of WWE. This thorough list displays his outstanding accomplishments within and beyond the squared circle.

WWE Championships:
- WWE Championship (16 times)
- World Heavyweight Championship (3 times)
- WWE United States Championship (5 times)

- WWE Tag Team Championship (2 times, with David Otunga and The Miz)

Royal Rumble Wins:
- Royal Rumble Match (2008, 2013)

Money in the Bank:
- WWE World Heavyweight Championship Money in the Bank (2012)

Notable Achievements:
- Sixteenth Grand Slam Champion in WWE history
- Fifth Triple Crown Champion in WWE history
- Longest reigning WWE Champion of the 2000s

- Fourth most world titles in WWE history

Appendix B: Filmography and Television Appearances

John Cena's move from the wrestling arena to the silver screen has been nothing short of amazing. This appendix summarises his noteworthy film and television projects, displaying his flexibility as a performer and his ambition to thrive in numerous entertainment genres.

Filmography:

- The Marine (2006) Cena's debut in main roles, demonstrating his action star potential.

- Trainwreck (2015)   A comedy role that enabled Cena to demonstrate his comic timing.
- Bumblebee (2018)   Cena's entry into big budget films, establishing his position in Hollywood.
- Blockers (2018)   A humorous role that emphasised his ability to connect with various audiences.
- Playing with Fire (2019)   Further development of Cena's comic abilities in a family friendly scenario.
- F9: The Fast Saga (2021)   Joining the Fast & Furious series, demonstrating his action talents.

Television Appearances:

- Saturday Night Live (2007, 2016) Hosting stints that emphasised Cena's charm and comic flair.

- Total Divas (2013) Guest appearances as himself, revealing insight into his personal life.

- American Grit (2016) Hosting a reality competition series that stressed mental and physical toughness.

- Wipeout (2021) Hosting the resurrection of the legendary obstacle course game program.

Appendix C: Selected Memorable Matches and Moments

John Cena's wrestling career is marked by several notable bouts and situations that have left an unforgettable impression on the WWE Universe. This addendum revisits a selection of these legendary meetings and segments that have contributed to Cena's enduring reputation.

Memorable Matches:
- John Cena vs. Shawn Michaels (WrestleMania 23, 2007) A great battle between two generational superstars.
- John Cena vs. CM Punk (Money in the Bank 2011) A modern day classic that featured narrative and in ring skill.

- John Cena vs. The Rock (WrestleMania 28, 2012) A once in a lifetime clash between two megastars.
- John Cena vs. AJ Styles (Royal Rumble 2017) A battle of styles that emphasised Cena's flexibility.
- John Cena vs. Bray Wyatt (WrestleMania 30, 2014) About that showcased Cena's commitment to promoting rising talents.

Iconic Moments:
- Debuting as the "Doctor of Thuganomics" , Cena's charming rap character laid the scene for his breakthrough.
- The "Ruthless Aggression" Promo Cena's challenge to WWE veterans

that signified a turning point in his career.

- Throwing his "Never Give Up" wristband to a little fan was a moving gesture that epitomised Cena's bond with his fans.

- The "Spinner" WWE Championship Introducing a modified championship that became iconic with his reigns.

- Surprise comeback Cena's surprise comeback regularly energised the audience, indicating his continuing popularity.

Plan Your Day

So You Do Not Forget What's Important

Day:

TO-DO

- [ ] _____
- [ ] _____
- [ ] _____
- [ ] _____
- [ ] _____
- [ ] _____
- [ ] _____
- [ ] _____
- [ ] _____
- [ ] _____
- [ ] _____
- [ ] _____
- [ ] _____
- [ ] _____
- [ ] _____
- [ ] _____
- [ ] _____
- [ ] _____
- [ ] _____

PRIORITIES

- [ ]
- [ ]
- [ ]
- [ ]
- [ ]
- [ ]
- [ ]
- [ ]
- [ ]

NOTES

Day:

TO-DO

- [ ] _____
- [ ] _____
- [ ] _____
- [ ] _____
- [ ] _____
- [ ] _____
- [ ] _____
- [ ] _____
- [ ] _____
- [ ] _____
- [ ] _____
- [ ] _____
- [ ] _____
- [ ] _____
- [ ] _____
- [ ] _____
- [ ] _____
- [ ] _____
- [ ] _____
- [ ] _____

PRIORITIES

- [ ]
- [ ]
- [ ]
- [ ]
- [ ]
- [ ]
- [ ]
- [ ]
- [ ]

NOTES

Day:

TO-DO

- [ ] _____
- [ ] _____
- [ ] _____
- [ ] _____
- [ ] _____
- [ ] _____
- [ ] _____
- [ ] _____
- [ ] _____
- [ ] _____
- [ ] _____
- [ ] _____
- [ ] _____
- [ ] _____
- [ ] _____
- [ ] _____
- [ ] _____
- [ ] _____
- [ ] _____
- [ ] _____

PRIORITIES

- [ ]
- [ ]
- [ ]
- [ ]
- [ ]
- [ ]
- [ ]
- [ ]
- [ ]

NOTES

Day:

TO-DO

- ☐ _____
- ☐ _____
- ☐ _____
- ☐ _____
- ☐ _____
- ☐ _____
- ☐ _____
- ☐ _____
- ☐ _____
- ☐ _____
- ☐ _____
- ☐ _____
- ☐ _____
- ☐ _____
- ☐ _____
- ☐ _____
- ☐ _____
- ☐ _____
- ☐ _____
- ☐ _____

PRIORITIES

- ☐
- ☐
- ☐
- ☐
- ☐
- ☐
- ☐
- ☐
- ☐

NOTES

Day:

TO-DO

☐ _____
☐ _____
☐ _____
☐ _____
☐ _____
☐ _____
☐ _____
☐ _____
☐ _____
☐ _____
☐ _____
☐ _____
☐ _____
☐ _____
☐ _____
☐ _____
☐ _____
☐ _____
☐ _____

PRIORITIES

☐
☐
☐
☐
☐
☐
☐
☐
☐

NOTES

Day:

TO-DO

☐ _____
☐ _____
☐ _____
☐ _____
☐ _____
☐ _____
☐ _____
☐ _____
☐ _____
☐ _____
☐ _____
☐ _____
☐ _____
☐ _____
☐ _____
☐ _____
☐ _____
☐ _____
☐ _____
☐ _____

PRIORITIES

☐
☐
☐
☐
☐
☐
☐
☐
☐

NOTES

Day:

TO-DO

- ☐ _____
- ☐ _____
- ☐ _____
- ☐ _____
- ☐ _____
- ☐ _____
- ☐ _____
- ☐ _____
- ☐ _____
- ☐ _____
- ☐ _____
- ☐ _____
- ☐ _____
- ☐ _____
- ☐ _____
- ☐ _____
- ☐ _____
- ☐ _____
- ☐ _____

PRIORITIES

- ☐
- ☐
- ☐
- ☐
- ☐
- ☐
- ☐
- ☐
- ☐

NOTES

Day:

TO-DO

- [ ] _____
- [ ] _____
- [ ] _____
- [ ] _____
- [ ] _____
- [ ] _____
- [ ] _____
- [ ] _____
- [ ] _____
- [ ] _____
- [ ] _____
- [ ] _____
- [ ] _____
- [ ] _____
- [ ] _____
- [ ] _____
- [ ] _____
- [ ] _____
- [ ] _____
- [ ] _____

PRIORITIES

- [ ]
- [ ]
- [ ]
- [ ]
- [ ]
- [ ]
- [ ]
- [ ]
- [ ]

NOTES

Day:

TO-DO

☐ _____
☐ _____
☐ _____
☐ _____
☐ _____
☐ _____
☐ _____
☐ _____
☐ _____
☐ _____
☐ _____
☐ _____
☐ _____
☐ _____
☐ _____
☐ _____
☐ _____
☐ _____
☐ _____
☐ _____

PRIORITIES

☐
☐
☐
☐
☐
☐
☐
☐
☐

NOTES

Day:

TO-DO

- [ ] _____
- [ ] _____
- [ ] _____
- [ ] _____
- [ ] _____
- [ ] _____
- [ ] _____
- [ ] _____
- [ ] _____
- [ ] _____
- [ ] _____
- [ ] _____
- [ ] _____
- [ ] _____
- [ ] _____
- [ ] _____
- [ ] _____
- [ ] _____
- [ ] _____
- [ ] _____
- [ ] _____

PRIORITIES

- [ ]
- [ ]
- [ ]
- [ ]
- [ ]
- [ ]
- [ ]
- [ ]
- [ ]

NOTES

Day:

TO-DO

- ☐ _____
- ☐ _____
- ☐ _____
- ☐ _____
- ☐ _____
- ☐ _____
- ☐ _____
- ☐ _____
- ☐ _____
- ☐ _____
- ☐ _____
- ☐ _____
- ☐ _____
- ☐ _____
- ☐ _____
- ☐ _____
- ☐ _____
- ☐ _____
- ☐ _____

PRIORITIES

- ☐
- ☐
- ☐
- ☐
- ☐
- ☐
- ☐
- ☐
- ☐

NOTES

Day:

TO-DO

- ☐ _____
- ☐ _____
- ☐ _____
- ☐ _____
- ☐ _____
- ☐ _____
- ☐ _____
- ☐ _____
- ☐ _____
- ☐ _____
- ☐ _____
- ☐ _____
- ☐ _____
- ☐ _____
- ☐ _____
- ☐ _____
- ☐ _____
- ☐ _____
- ☐ _____
- ☐ _____

PRIORITIES

- ☐
- ☐
- ☐
- ☐
- ☐
- ☐
- ☐
- ☐
- ☐

NOTES

Day:

TO-DO

- [ ] _____
- [ ] _____
- [ ] _____
- [ ] _____
- [ ] _____
- [ ] _____
- [ ] _____
- [ ] _____
- [ ] _____
- [ ] _____
- [ ] _____
- [ ] _____
- [ ] _____
- [ ] _____
- [ ] _____
- [ ] _____
- [ ] _____
- [ ] _____
- [ ] _____
- [ ] _____

PRIORITIES

- [ ]
- [ ]
- [ ]
- [ ]
- [ ]
- [ ]
- [ ]
- [ ]
- [ ]

NOTES

Day:

TO-DO

- [ ] _____
- [ ] _____
- [ ] _____
- [ ] _____
- [ ] _____
- [ ] _____
- [ ] _____
- [ ] _____
- [ ] _____
- [ ] _____
- [ ] _____
- [ ] _____
- [ ] _____
- [ ] _____
- [ ] _____
- [ ] _____
- [ ] _____
- [ ] _____
- [ ] _____
- [ ] _____

PRIORITIES

- [ ]
- [ ]
- [ ]
- [ ]
- [ ]
- [ ]
- [ ]
- [ ]
- [ ]

NOTES

Day:

TO-DO

- ☐ _____
- ☐ _____
- ☐ _____
- ☐ _____
- ☐ _____
- ☐ _____
- ☐ _____
- ☐ _____
- ☐ _____
- ☐ _____
- ☐ _____
- ☐ _____
- ☐ _____
- ☐ _____
- ☐ _____
- ☐ _____
- ☐ _____
- ☐ _____
- ☐ _____
- ☐ _____

PRIORITIES

- ☐
- ☐
- ☐
- ☐
- ☐
- ☐
- ☐
- ☐
- ☐

NOTES

Day:

TO-DO

- [ ] _____
- [ ] _____
- [ ] _____
- [ ] _____
- [ ] _____
- [ ] _____
- [ ] _____
- [ ] _____
- [ ] _____
- [ ] _____
- [ ] _____
- [ ] _____
- [ ] _____
- [ ] _____
- [ ] _____
- [ ] _____
- [ ] _____
- [ ] _____
- [ ] _____

PRIORITIES

- [ ]
- [ ]
- [ ]
- [ ]
- [ ]
- [ ]
- [ ]
- [ ]
- [ ]

NOTES

Day:

TO-DO

- [ ] _____
- [ ] _____
- [ ] _____
- [ ] _____
- [ ] _____
- [ ] _____
- [ ] _____
- [ ] _____
- [ ] _____
- [ ] _____
- [ ] _____
- [ ] _____
- [ ] _____
- [ ] _____
- [ ] _____
- [ ] _____
- [ ] _____
- [ ] _____
- [ ] _____
- [ ] _____

PRIORITIES

- [ ]
- [ ]
- [ ]
- [ ]
- [ ]
- [ ]
- [ ]
- [ ]
- [ ]

NOTES

Day:

TO-DO

- [ ] _____
- [ ] _____
- [ ] _____
- [ ] _____
- [ ] _____
- [ ] _____
- [ ] _____
- [ ] _____
- [ ] _____
- [ ] _____
- [ ] _____
- [ ] _____
- [ ] _____
- [ ] _____
- [ ] _____
- [ ] _____
- [ ] _____
- [ ] _____
- [ ] _____
- [ ] _____
- [ ] _____

PRIORITIES

- [ ]
- [ ]
- [ ]
- [ ]
- [ ]
- [ ]
- [ ]
- [ ]
- [ ]

NOTES

Day:

TO-DO

- ☐ _____
- ☐ _____
- ☐ _____
- ☐ _____
- ☐ _____
- ☐ _____
- ☐ _____
- ☐ _____
- ☐ _____
- ☐ _____
- ☐ _____
- ☐ _____
- ☐ _____
- ☐ _____
- ☐ _____
- ☐ _____
- ☐ _____
- ☐ _____
- ☐ _____

PRIORITIES

- ☐
- ☐
- ☐
- ☐
- ☐
- ☐
- ☐
- ☐
- ☐

NOTES

Day:

TO-DO

- ☐ _____
- ☐ _____
- ☐ _____
- ☐ _____
- ☐ _____
- ☐ _____
- ☐ _____
- ☐ _____
- ☐ _____
- ☐ _____
- ☐ _____
- ☐ _____
- ☐ _____
- ☐ _____
- ☐ _____
- ☐ _____
- ☐ _____
- ☐ _____
- ☐ _____
- ☐ _____

PRIORITIES

- ☐
- ☐
- ☐
- ☐
- ☐
- ☐
- ☐
- ☐
- ☐

NOTES

Printed in Great Britain
by Amazon

34761399R00061